Pebble® Plus

PIRATES AHOY!

Pirate Treasure

by Rosalyn Tucker

Consulting editor: Gail Saunders-Smith, PhD

raintree

a Capstone company — publishers for children

Raintree is an imprint of Capstone Global Library Limited, a company incorporated in England and Wales having its registered office at 7 Pilgrim Street, London, EC4V 6LB – Registered company number: 6695582

www.raintree.co.uk
myorders@raintree.co.uk

Text © Capstone Global Library Limited 2015
The moral rights of the proprietor have been asserted.

Editorial Credits
Michelle Hasselius, editor; Kazuko Collins, designer; Gina Kammer, media researcher; Gene Bentdahl, production specialist

ISBN 978 1 406 29353 1
19 18 17 16 15
10 9 8 7 6 5 4 3 2 1

British Library Cataloguing in Publication Data
A full catalogue record for this book is available from the British Library.

Photo Credits
Bridgeman Images: Look and Learn/Private Collection/Life below deck (gouache on paper), Rainer, Paul (20th century), 11, Look and Learn/Private Collection/Pirates landing at harbour, McBride, Angus (1931–2007), 13; Getty Images: Archive Photos/PhotoQuest, 15, McClatchy-Tribune/MCT/Chicago Tribune, 21, National Geographic/Emory Kristof, 19; North Wind Picture Archives, 5, 7, 17; Shutterstock: Chantal de Bruijne, 9, David Spieth (beach), cover, Fer Gregory (treasure chest), cover
Design elements: Shutterstock: A-R-T (old paper), La Gorda (rope illustration), vovan (old wood)

Printed in China by Nordica.
0914/CA21401504

Contents

Pirates in the Golden Age

Dangerous pirates looked for treasure during the Golden Age of Piracy (1690–1730).

Pirates attacked other ships at sea.

They stole the treasures on board.

Pirate Jean Lafitte with a treasure chest

Before aeroplanes and trains, ships carried goods to other parts of the world. Ships were filled with items such as gold and jewels. These treasures were worth a lot of money to a pirate.

English ships carried goods across the sea.

Types of treasure

Most people think pirates wanted only gold and jewels. But everyday items were just as valuable. Pirates stole ropes, ship sails and tools. They could use these items on their ships.

ropes and tools used at sea

Even people were a type of treasure. Pirates forced men to work on their ships. Doctors took care of sick or hurt pirates. Skilled workers mended ships.

Pirate crews had to work hard on ships.

Selling riches

Few pirates kept their treasures for very long. They wanted money instead. Many pirates sold their stolen goods in nearby towns.

Pirates sold stolen goods at low prices.

Wealthy people wanted their own pieces of pirate treasure. They bought statues or silk fans from pirates. These treasures were displayed in the finest homes.

Wealthy people bought treasures from pirate William Kidd.

A few pirates buried their treasures. William Kidd buried his gold on an island. Most of his treasure has never been found.

William Kidd buried his treasure on Gardiners Island in New York, USA in 1699.

Pirate treasure today

Scientists study pirate treasure
to learn about pirate life. These
items can tell us how pirates
lived and where they sailed.

Divers found treasure on the Spanish ship *San Diego*. The ship sank in the 1600s.

Pirate treasures are displayed in

museums around the world. But

not all treasures have been found.

People still search for treasure today.

pirate treasure at the Field
Museum in Chicago, USA

Glossary

attack try to hurt someone or something

display show something

Golden Age of Piracy period from 1690 to 1730, when thousands of people became pirates around the world

goods items that can be bought or sold

pirate person who steals from ships and towns

scientist person who studies the world around him or her

statue model of a person or animal made from metal, stone or wood

treasure gold, jewels, money and other items of value

valuable something that is worth a lot of money or is very important

Books

The Great Big Book of Pirates, John Malam (QED Publishing, 2008)

Pirates (Legends of the Sea), Rebecca Rissman (Raintree, 2011)

Pirate Things to Make and Do (Usborne Activities), Rebecca Gilpin (Usborne Publishing, 2011)

Websites

www.nationalgeographic.com/features/97/pirates
Play interactive games and learn fun facts about daring pirates who sailed the seas.

www.bbc.co.uk/cbeebies/swashbuckle-online/games
Find the treasure and make the pirates walk the plank! Try these fun pirate games.

Index